Vernon Johnson

Revised and updated by Donal Foley

All booklets are published
thanks to the generosity of the supporters
of the Catholic Truth Society

Contents

 First published 2008 by The Incorporated Catholic Truth Society 40-46 Harleyford Road, London SE11 5AY Tel: 020 7640 0042 Fax: 020 7640 0046.

ISBN 978 1 86082 486 9

Message of Lourdes

Suffering is something which modern men and women, including many Catholics, find very difficult to endure, or even to understand. "What is the point of it?" they say. "Why would a good God allow us to suffer?" In the past people largely accepted suffering, and even today, in the developing world, suffering is a part of life for many. But the whole trend of modern Western civilisation is to want to do away with pain and suffering, to rebel against them, even though experience should have taught us by now that suffering is inevitable in our world.

The Christian answer to the problem of pain and suffering, however, is that suffering, while not a good thing in itself does have a meaning and a purpose, and that, rightly understood and accepted, it can be a powerful impetus in our journey towards God. This was one of the underlying messages which emerged from the apparitions at Lourdes in 1858, not least through the life of Bernadette

Soubirous, the seer of Lourdes, who endured so much suffering in her comparatively short life.

Lourdes, through the spring uncovered by Bernadette, became a great centre for pilgrimages for the sick, and was also the scene of many miraculous cures; but it is also an implicit reminder through the messages of Our Lady, and through Bernadette's heroic witness, of the fact that the sufferings of Christ during his crucifixion were an essential part of God's plan for the redemption of mankind. We should also realise too that St Paul had said that he was happy to suffer in his own body to make up for what still had to be undergone by Christ for the sake of his Church (*Col* 1:24), a statement which indicates that the Mystical Body of Christ, that is all Christians, must also expect to suffer if we are to be truly like Christ.

True healing and happiness

The vast majority of the sick people who have gone to Lourdes have not been cured, and yet the grace to accept their sufferings and offer them up lovingly to God will have been freely available to them: all that is necessary is to ask for it with faith. Despite the tremendous medical advances which have taken place since the nineteenth century, there are still many diseases which medical science is unable to deal with adequately. And this is to say nothing of the huge growth in emotional problems which affect so many in the West today. Thus we have a situation where many people are still desperately in need of healing, and perhaps in most cases are more in need of emotional than physical healing. And it is undoubtedly the case that we are *all* in need of spiritual healing to some degree or other. Thus although medical science has found a way to deal with many illnesses, the essential message of Lourdes and St Bernadette, that only by turning to God with a humble and contrite heart can we find true healing and true happiness, is no less timely today than it was one hundred and fifty years ago.

The business of being ill

We can imagine that we have at last arrived as pilgrims at Lourdes. It has been a long and tiring journey, and for some it might have a painful one; but we have been supported by our eagerness to reach the Grotto where Our Blessed Lady appeared to Bernadette.

And now we are at the very spot where St Bernadette knelt and talked with Mary, looking up at the very Grotto where Our Lady herself appeared.

This is a good moment to review the story of these apparitions.

At Lourdes

Bernadette, a little girl intellectually backward and physically ill, left her home one day in Lourdes, in February 1858, to gather sticks by the side of the River Gave, because they were too poor at home to afford coal for their fire. In reality, her home was little more than a hovel; they lived in an old disused prison.

As she and her brother and sister came along the riverbank, they reached a canal. Bernadette, fearing the cold water, was afraid to cross. Her brother and sister laughed at her and left her behind. Bernadette stooped down to remove her stockings, when suddenly she heard the sound of wind in the trees and looking up she saw the Blessed Virgin Mary in the Grotto surrounded by a golden light. Bernadette fell on her knees. Our Lady appeared thus to Bernadette eighteen times and gave her a number of messages. She told her that she wished people to come there in procession and to do penance both for themselves and for others. She told her to make a hole in the sand, and water flowed forth.

Many years have passed, and this grotto, then unknown, is one of the best known and most loved places in the Catholic world. Miracles of healing have taken place through the spring of water which was unsealed at the touch of Bernadette's hand. The history of Lourdes has been one of uninterrupted glory. Millions have come here in procession to do penance. The world thinks only of the physical miracles, but the Church values as far more precious those supernatural healings of the soul which take place here: those marvelous workings of grace in the soul by which the sick who come here and are not cured return home accepting this and perhaps regarding their sufferings as their most precious treasure. This is Lourdes' greatest gift for those prepared to accept it. And the instrument chosen by Our Lord to bring all this about was little Bernadette, weak and frail.

At Nevers

While Lourdes was passing from glory to glory, however, where was Bernadette? Hidden in her convent at Nevers in central France: stricken with sickness. What was she doing? One day some visitors asked her if she had heard of some of the recent wonders of Lourdes. She answered no. The visitors could not understand how this could be. Bernadette replied, "You see, my business is to be ill."

Why was it her business? Because it was through sickness that Our Lord had ordained that Bernadette should save her soul. Bernadette did not become a saint because she saw Our Lady and talked with her. She became a saint through her willing acceptance of sickness and suffering in the silence of the convent of Nevers. It was her business to be ill because it was the business given to her directly from heaven. She suffered very greatly and died a painful death; and that suffering and death made her a saint and was her path straight to heaven, because she accepted it as her business, sent to her direct from her heavenly Father. And therefore it was her greatest treasure.

This was something Bernadette had understood from the beginning: the Blessed Virgin had said to her during one apparition that she was not promising her happiness in this world, but the next, while her admonitions on other occasions, including, "Pray for sinners," "Penance! Penance! Penance!" and "Kiss the ground as a penance for sinners," clearly indicated the path that Bernadette would have to take.

Illness

Towards the end of her life, in 1875, Bernadette had advised a young novice that she "must learn to love suffering. Our Lord gives His crown of thorns to his

Incorrupt body of St Bernadette at Nevers.

friends. Seek nothing better." On another occasion she said, "the more I am crucified, the more I rejoice".

In this she was only speaking from experience. From this time on she was almost constantly ill, confined to bed, and suffering greatly. Even from her earliest years at Nevers she had been a victim of a tubercular condition of the right knee, but this developed into an abscess in 1877 which left her in constant and agonizing pain. In 1879 she became much weaker, was hardly able to eat and became quite emaciated. She was also tormented by painful sores on all her limbs. On 28th March she was anointed for the fourth and final time, dying on 16th April after a long and painful last agony.

When we are ill

Sometimes, we too have to accept suffering and illness. Most of the sick who return home from Lourdes are not cured: it is also their "business" to be ill. Although we often find it hard to believe and even harder to accept, sickness and suffering are very precious, even though suffering is not something that is good in itself. Although she suffered a great deal, St Bernadette was not a masochist. In December 1878, a few months before her death, when she was confined to bed, a fellow sister noticed an image of St Bernard, her patron, nearby, and asked her about it. Bernadette responded that she prayed to him, "but I don't imitate him at all. St Bernard loved suffering. I avoid it as much as I can."

Holiness

However, for those with very serious illnesses, it may well be that suffering is the way the heavenly Father means them to become saints and enter heaven. And that is the only thing that really matters. What is the whole world worth to us if we do not have the hope of heaven, with Our Lord, Our Lady and all the saints to welcome us? As St Therese of Lisieux, who was proclaimed a Doctor of the Church by Pope John Paul II, said: "Sanctity lies not in saying beautiful things, or even in thinking them, or feeling them; it lies in truly being willing to suffer."

So for some people it may well be their business is to be ill, to be like Bernadette or Therese, to suffer with Our Lord, to be caught up by their suffering into a tender and intimate communion with the pierced and broken heart of our Divine Saviour.

There is no other way to heaven except suffering, whether in this world or in purgatory. Our Blessed

Lord saved the world and opened heaven to us through suffering. The more we suffer with Him, the greater chance we have of becoming saints.

The teaching of the saints

This was the teaching of St Vincent de Paul, who said: "If we only knew the precious treasure hidden in infirmities, we would receive them with the same joy with which we receive the greatest benefits, and we would bear them without ever complaining or showing signs of weariness." More recently, St Faustina in her *Diary* wrote: "Oh, if only the suffering soul knew how much God loves it, it would die of joy and excess of happiness! Someday, we will know the value of suffering, but then we will no longer be able to suffer. The present moment is ours."

We may have a friend who has never suffered. What do we say of him? We say, "Oh, he is very charming, but everything has gone well with him so far." And that little word *but* reveals the fact that all of us know deep down: that it is only in the hour of suffering and trial that the deepest things in men and women are called forth, either for good or for evil.

The Way of Love

Thus we have to try and understand that suffering taken from God as God's business for us will make us saints.

The Reverend Mother of the convent of Nevers was waiting at the convent door. In front of her stood little Bernadette, about whom the whole Catholic world at the time was talking. The Reverend Mother moved forward to receive her as a postulant to the community and questioned her as to her gifts. "What can you do?" she asked her. Bernadette looked up at her and made this exquisite reply: "Nothing very much." The sheer beauty of that answer! Think of it. "Nothing very much"!

That is how Bernadette became a saint, by doing nothing very much extraordinarily well; and that is how all saints are made.

Perhaps the supreme modern example of this has been St Therese of Lisieux. Her whole spirituality was built on her 'Little Way' of love, which involved nothing more than a full realisation that she was a child of the Heavenly Father, a little child totally dependent on Him for everything. A little child does not attempt to do great things which it knows are beyond its strength. Rather it is content to do small acts for its parents, but with much love. The Little Way is also the way of humility, which makes us recognise how much we depend on God, and opens us up to His grace. So St Therese offered up little acts of love to God, comprised of all the incidents, problems and difficulties of her life, as well as its joys; but she did this so well that this was enough for Pope Pius X to proclaim her the "greatest saint of modern times."

Little by little

Like Bernadette, Therese also had much to suffer towards the end of her life, but abandoned herself completely to God: "I thank you, O my God, for all the graces you have bestowed on me, and particularly for having made me pass through the crucible of suffering." Shortly before she died she said: "Never would I have believed it was possible to suffer so much!"

In all this she was only echoing the teaching of the great Carmelite Doctor of the Church, St John of the Cross, who said: "I would like to persuade spiritual persons that the way to perfection does not consist of many methods nor much thinking, but in denying oneself in everything and suffering for the love of Jesus Christ."

It may well be that through our particular, perhaps severe, sufferings we have been called to become saints. We naturally ask: "How is it to be done?" Well, not by being ready-made magnificent martyrs of pain - no, but by just taking the little things and doing nothing very much extraordinarily well. This means that to become a saint is possible for anyone in such a situation. Even if they realise that they can do "nothing very much", aided by grace, they can do this extraordinarily well.

How God works

Now look how God has done extraordinarily well through nothing very much. He wished to come down to earth as man. Whom did he choose? A royal queen, clothed in purple with a crown of gold on her head, surrounded by great magnificence and by men and women of great renown? No; he chose a humble maiden of Nazareth, a little town hidden in the silence of the Galilean hills. He did not choose very much as the world counts its values.

He wanted to come into the world in our human nature. Was the Sacred Humanity fashioned in a moment, through the seraphim and cherubim, and mankind thus forced to its knees? No; he came as a tiny baby. Nothing very much, as the world would say.

He wants to feed you with himself - he wants to give you himself and all the power of his love - he has come down to earth, not only in Bethlehem but somewhere else. Where? In some mighty, glorious manifestation? No; in the Blessed Sacrament. Nothing very much to look at. God is apparently doing nothing very much when, at the words of the priest, he comes down to earth under the appearance of the frail white Host. And yet in that blessed mystery there is the whole of the Godhead.

Through nothing very much - that is how God works. He takes things that seem nothing and fills them with the supernatural, and makes the smallest thing he touches greater than the greatest things that are outside that supernatural touch. We may have magnificent health, but if we never think of God, it is useless in God's eyes. We may have great gifts, but if they are not touched with the supernatural, they can do nothing in the supernatural order at all.

It is the little things, packed full of the supernatural love of God, that turn the world upside down. A baby in the cradle at Bethlehem, the Blessed Sacrament on the altar, little Bernadette kneeling in the grotto at Lourdes. These are the things God takes.

People rush to see the latest attraction, or to sit rapt before the television watching the latest media star. "He (or she) is so marvelous," they cry. The person who is suffering is often ignored, and yet that unimportant person, by offering their pain to Jesus, is doing more good in the world than all the most brilliant media stars can ever do. As St John of the Cross said in his *Spiritual Canticle*: "The smallest act of pure love is of greater value to the Church than all other works united together."

"Nothing very much," said Bernadette, and yet millions still go to Lourdes, finding it a place of life, healing and strength.

Accepting Suffering

For some people then, it may well be that it is their business is to be ill; that is the vocation God has given them, because that is the way God means them to be one of his saints.

We will become saints by learning the value of very little things. The little things make or break us. Suppose we were going back home uncured after Lourdes to the same difficulties, the same little irritations and annoyances. If seriously ill, the same people would be looking after us - who, although they love us dearly, often do little things that get on our nerves. Even minor illnesses can be very irritating.

But instead of these things worrying us and irritating us, we can *decide* to accept them quietly and gladly because they are amongst the things that are going to make us into saints.

Suffering and holiness

We can offer to Jesus every one of these countless little things which seem such thorns. We can make each one a little offering of our love, and he will take it and unite it to his Cross, and each thorn will become a rose. And Jesus may well take our offering and use it to make someone else's pain easier to bear.

That is how we can use pain and suffering to become saints. By being ill, by offering all our little pains with the pain of the Son of God and so becoming saints little by little. Nothing dramatic or startling, nothing very much as the world thinks, but in reality each one a little step by which we mount the ladder of holiness till we see God face to face. This ladder is the way to heaven for all of us at some time or other.

Fatima children

And in fact, this is a lesson which God, through the lives of the saints of recent times, seems to be particularly emphasising for the Church today. We can see this if we look at some examples. Jacinta and Francisco Marto, the two youngest of the three seers of the apparitions at Fatima in Portugal in 1917, who died while still children, certainly had to suffer a great deal. Even Sr Lucia, the oldest seer, who became a Carmelite nun, suffered quite acutely towards the end of her very long life.

Francisco Marto

Following the apparitions, an influenza epidemic swept Europe in autumn of 1918, just as the First World War was ending, and both Jacinta and Francisco fell ill. Francisco recovered somewhat and there were hopes that he might become well, but his condition worsened again. He offered up all his sufferings as a way of consoling God for the sinfulness and ingratitude of mankind, becoming so weak that eventually he could not even pray. Lucia visited him noting that he always appeared joyful and content despite his illness. She asked him if he was suffering a lot, to which he replied: "Quite a lot, but never mind! I am suffering to console Our Lord, and afterwards, within a short time, I am going to heaven!" He received his first Holy Communion, and on the next day, 4th April 1919, he died, aged only ten.

Jacinta Marto

Jacinta too was confined to her bed, and although she recovered was struck down with bronchial pneumonia, while also developing a painful abscess in her chest. She was moved to a nearby hospital in

July 1919, where she underwent the painful treatment prescribed for her, but without much effect. Lucia likewise visited her, asking her if she was suffering a lot. She replied: "Yes, I am. But I offer everything for sinners and in reparation to the Immaculate Heart of Mary." Lucia comments that Jacinta was "filled with enthusiasm" as she spoke of Our Lord and Our Lady: "Oh, how much I love to suffer for love of Them, just to give Them pleasure! They greatly love those who suffer for the conversion of sinners."

Jacinta returned home in August with an open wound in her side, but it was decided that another attempt should be made to treat her, and so in January 1920 she was taken to Lisbon, where she was diagnosed as having purulent pleurisy and diseased ribs. Eventually in February she was admitted into hospital, where she underwent another painful operation to remove two ribs; this left her with a large wound in her side that had to be dressed daily, causing her agony. On the evening of 20th February the local priest was called and heard her Confession, but he insisted on waiting till the next day to bring her Communion, despite her protests that she felt worse; and so she died that night alone, aged only nine, and far from her family. Jacinta and Francisco were both beatified by Pope John Paul II in 2000.

Shoulder your Cross

It's striking how, like Bernadette, the children of Fatima suffered so much, and this indicates one of the underlying themes of the modern apparitions of Mary, that we do have to be prepared to suffer if we are to take up our cross every day, and follow in the footsteps of Christ and his Mother. And of course the sufferings of Jacinta and Francisco have borne marvelous fruit in the worldwide propagation of the Fatima message and particularly in the collegial consecration of Russia to Mary's Immaculate Heart which was carried out by John Paul II in 1984, in union with a moral totality of the world's bishops.

Alexandrina de Costa

Another person who suffered greatly for Christ during the twentieth century was Alexandrina da Costa, who like Jacinta and Francisco was Portuguese. Indeed her mission was so closely linked to theirs spiritually that she has been described as the "fourth seer of Fatima." She gradually became incapacitated and confined to bed after jumping from a window to escape from a man who wanted to molest her. She offered herself as a victim to Our Lord to make reparation for the sins of mankind, enduring great sufferings, and from March

1942 until her death in October 1955 she lived solely on daily Holy Communion. She was declared Venerable by Pope John Paul II in January 1996.

Marthe Robin

Likewise, Marthe Robin, who was born in 1902, and lived in southeastern France, gradually became paralysed as she grew older, and in October 1930, received the stigmata and began to undergo the Passion of Christ each Friday every week until her death in 1981. Like Alexandrina she was confined to bed, and offered up her sufferings in reparation. Despite being paralysed, she was able, with Fr Georges Finet, to become the co-foundress of the Foyers of Charity; these are communities of lay persons headed by a priest, the Father of the Foyer, who is responsible for preaching five day silent retreats.

Even as early as 1936, Marthe foresaw a new Pentecost of Love, which would be preceded by a renewal of the Church which would come about mainly through the laity. Thus she anticipated the Second Vatican Council and the work of the Popes since John XXIII. In addition, her Cause has been introduced at Rome, while there are now more than 70 Foyer communities around the world. This is surely a great example of the how God can use suffering in a 'creative' and positive way, to build up the Church.

Like Bernadette, Marthe was a great lover of the rosary, and was also very much influenced by the Marian teachings of St Louis de Montfort. She also lived the 'Little Way' of St Therese, and in fact the Carmelite Saint, who had been canonised in 1925, actually appeared to her on three separate occasions telling her that she would carry on her mission and make it more universal. Around this time Marthe noted that "suffering is the best school in which to learn true love." She also said that, "Of all the forms of the apostolate, that of good works, that of prayer, that of example, that of suffering, this last apostolate is worth the most; and prayer, like good works, only acquires its fruitfulness in sacrifice." Like Alexandrina, Marthe lived solely on the Eucharist which she received only once a week, and similarly both were humble and anxious to avoid publicity or draw attention to themselves.

We might say that both Alexandrina and Marthe were 'extreme' cases and that the majority of Christians are not called to live such lives of suffering and this is true; but equally, if they could suffer a lot, can we not suffer a little for the love of Christ?

John Paul II

Many others have suffered greatly in modern times, including St Pio of Pietrelcina and St Maximilian Kolbe, to say nothing of all the martyrs under Communism and Nazism, but perhaps it is the life and sufferings of Pope John Paul II which have had the most impact recently. When he was elected Pope in 1978 he was a vigorous man of 58, an intellectual but also an athletic figure, in good health and keen on activities such as skiing and hiking. But gradually, as he grew older, the cares of Office began to take their toll, and this process accelerated following the attempt on his life in 1981.

In 1984 he wrote the encyclical letter *Salvifici Doloris* which was concerned with how the Church understood the meaning of suffering. It focused on three aspects: firstly, that suffering can be seen as having a creative value, that is that God can bring good even out of evil; secondly that it also has a saving or salvific value, that is that we can suffer for Christ and with Christ; and finally, it dealt with how believers should respond towards suffering, that is to see it as a way of living out their baptismal vocation, to become co-workers in the saving mission of Christ.

It could be said that John Paul II eventually lived out the teaching found in this letter, because towards the end of his life he was only a shadow of his former self; and yet he did not allow his sufferings, which included Parkinson's Disease, to cause him to swerve from his path of total dedication to Christ. Rather he saw them as the providential way by which he would give his final testimony to the world, that illness, pain, and even death have an ultimate meaning and are not useless in God's sight.

So these more modern saints and holy persons have echoed the teaching and example of St Bernadette, who, as we have seen, in her humility had said, "Nothing very much," when the Reverend Mother asked her what she could do. Like them, Bernadette was prepared to accept her sufferings as coming from the Hand of God, and this is something we mustn't forget.

What is Humility?

As Bernadette was dying and was about to receive the last sacraments, she turned to her sisters and said: "I ask my sisters to forgive me for the bad example I have set them." The simple beauty of it! She who has seen Our Lady, she who was chosen by God as the instrument of all the glory of Lourdes, as she lies dying, turns to her sisters and apologises for her life. "I ask my sisters to forgive me for the bad example I have set them."

The secret of holiness

Now, what is the meaning of these amazing words? Well, in them lies the secret of holiness. And the secret of holiness is humility. Surely, if anyone had the right to think herself fairly good, it was Bernadette, she who had seen Our Lady and to whom Our Lady herself had spoken. Yet she apologises for her bad example to her sisters.

It seems almost fantastic. Why? Because when we think of humility, we compare ourselves with somebody else, some of those around us, and we think: "Well, we're not quite so bad after all."

But in the case of Bernadette, the secret of her humility lay in the fact that she did not compare herself with any of her friends around her, but with the Lady who had appeared to her at the grotto. That is where she learned humility: in the presence of the spotless purity of Mary, she saw her own sinfulness; in the presence of Our Lady's absolute humility, she saw her own self-will and pride. And ever afterwards, having enjoyed these wonderful privileges, she did not think: "How much better I am than others," but she went through life apologising for her bad example.

Humility

What is humility? First of all, humility is seeing things as they really are, namely, that God is everything and that we, without him, are absolutely nothing. Our Blessed Lord has told us: "Cut off from me you can do nothing" (*Jn* 15:5).

But humility is more than this. Humility is seeing ourselves as we really are, namely, that we are a strange mixture of good and bad; for don't let us forget that we all have our good points. But humility shows us that all that is good in us is of God, and all that is bad is of Self.

Willing to learn

The moment the truly humble soul realises this, its one desire is to remove, by the help of grace, every single thing that is bad, so that the love of God may fill the soul and that there may not be a single corner where self-love and pride make it impossible for Jesus to live and reign. And so the humble soul will always be not merely willing but glad to learn its faults.

This is the supreme test. There is no other way in which humility can be learnt. Bernadette learnt humility because she was willing to see, to accept and to admit her faults. "I ask my sisters to forgive me for the bad example I have set them." That was the basis of her humility.

And so, there is really only one way for us to become humble. We must be glad to be told our faults. And we know quite well that that is one of the hardest things in the world. To be told our faults is such a humiliation. And yet if we desire to be humble we can see, can't we, that to be told our faults is really the greatest blessing. In fact, we can measure a person's holiness exactly by the way in which that person takes a humiliation. The ordinary person resents it and gets angry. The saint accepts it with joy.

Blessing in humiliations

Regardless of how much or little we are suffering, we all have to begin again the great work of becoming a saint through doing well the things God asks of us. And the secret of sanctity is just this: never to mind finding out that we are in the wrong; never to mind being treated in a way which humbles us; never to mind being misjudged, or being told that we have done something which perhaps we have never done or thought of; never to mind being misunderstood or neglected; never to mind being thought to be a nuisance or a burden - but just to see in all these humiliations the greatest possible blessing. Because these are the things that penetrate to the very depths of our self-love as nothing else can do. They show us how deeply rooted is our pride, and they teach us how much we need the help of grace if we are ever to be holy.

Ministering to others

The Grotto of Lourdes made Bernadette humble because it showed her what she was. And her story ought to make us grasp our sinfulness and need for humility. If we can realise these things we will have a great sense of our own needs before God, and therefore a deep compassion for the needs of others.

And for the person who is seriously ill, this deep knowledge will give them a wonderful compassion for those who minister to them. These ideas echo what St Therese had to say on this point: "I have noticed that the experience of suffering makes us kind and indulgent toward others because it is suffering that draws us near to God."

Suffering makes us realise what we really are - just poor, weak things, and that without God we simply could not bear our pain or anguish for one moment; without God we simply could not be good for one instant; without Our Blessed Lord we could not be patient for one day.

Each one of us ought to realise what a bad example we set; and then we shall ask God humbly to take us in his arms, to lift us up the ladder of holiness which we cannot climb ourselves, step by step, each step being a step of humility, a revelation of another fault in us. Let us place ourselves once again in the almighty arms of God, saying: "I can do nothing. You can do all. By myself I can only do harm, but in your arms I can become a saint." And so there will grow in us that same beautiful humility which was the secret of the holiness of Bernadette.

Humility of Bernadette

Humility is the foundation of all true greatness. Our Divine Saviour humbled himself to death, "even death on a cross. But God raised him high and gave him the name which is above all other names" (*Ph* 2:8-9).

What was it that drew Almighty God to make Mary his mother? It was her humility. "He has looked upon his lowly handmaid" (*Lk* 1:48). It was just because she was so humble that she became the Mother of God.

When Our Lady came to single out someone in Lourdes to whom she could confide the secrets of her Divine Son, whom did she choose? A little girl, Bernadette, so utterly humble that, although at the time of her death the whole Catholic world was thinking about her, and her fame had spread through every country in Europe, she died with these words on her lips: "I ask my sisters to forgive me for the bad example I have set them." It was the humility of Bernadette, not the wonders of Lourdes that made her the saint she is.

At Lourdes then, the Church, our mother, holds Bernadette in her arms as it were, and says; "The one who makes himself as little as this little child is the greatest in the kingdom of heaven" (*Mt* 18:4); just as her Divine Lord and Master said it so many years ago, when he too held a little one in his arms, and said: "Learn from me, for I am gentle and humble in heart, and you will find rest for your souls" (*Mt* 11:29).

The Cup He Has Given Us

We can also think about a very beautiful prayer which Saint Bernadette offered up during the last days of her long and weary illness.

As her sisters knelt round her bed they heard her praying, and this was the prayer they heard: "My God, it is your will. I accept the cup which you have given me. Blessed be your holy name." We could not have a more perfect prayer than this to ponder on, especially if we are suffering in any way. It is a prayer which will, in a most marvelous way, bring light and comfort to us. Let us consider it phrase by phrase.

'My God' - not just the word God, as it might be uttered by someone in despair or in rebellion against their fate, but 'my God', the God who is my Father, the God whose child I am. Our Lord told us this himself; when he rose from the grave his message of triumph was: "I am ascending to my Father and your Father, to my God and your God" (*Jn* 20:17).

The love of God

So 'my God' means the God who loves me as a father loves his child. That little word *my* tells me that the love of my Heavenly Father has been fixed on me from all eternity. From all eternity that spotlight of the love of God has been fixed upon my soul, fixed on me as though I was the only person in the world, following me as I move through life, from birth till death, and indeed through all eternity.

'My God' - that little word *my* shows that you matter intensely to the great God who made the whole wide world, just because he is your Father and you are his child.

Everything begins in God, everything is supported by God, everything ends in him; and he is love. He, then, is the only person who matters. What he wills is the only thing that can be really good for us. Therefore the prayer goes on: "My God, it is your will." There is nothing more to be said. "It is your will," and therefore it is the very best for me. Never mind what I might think was good for me; never mind what my will would desire. The only thing that matters is "your will", the will of the Father who loves me, his child. My will must disappear before this all-loving will of almighty God.

A father's gift

And so Saint Bernadette added: "I accept the cup which you have given me." She accepted her sickness, her long, weary illness, not because she was driven to it against her will, but because she freely grasped what she knew to be the best possible thing for her, the cup which her Father gave her. Her illness was to her the gift of a Father to his child; and so, with the perfect trust of a little one, she held out her trembling hands and gladly directed to her lips the chalice of suffering which her Heavenly Father gave her as his most precious gift. This is clear from what she said to a fellow sister in 1874: "Accept sickness as a caress. Spend your all in the service of the poor but prudently. Never let yourself give way to discouragement," and naturally enough, "Have real love for the holy Virgin."

We may have to follow in the steps of Bernadette. We may have in front of us many hours, days, weeks, months or even years of weary pain, but we do not have to accept this with bitterness just because we are compelled to do so. We can accept it as she did; we can stretch out our hand to grasp that cup of pain and suffering because it is his will for us, it is the special gift of him who is our Father to we who are his children.

Despite outward appearances, we can perhaps grasp why it is such a blessed gift. To share the cup with a friend means to share their most intimate life; it is a sign of fellowship, communion. And so we can see that a painful illness, which seems such a heavy cross, is indeed a Cross - but it is the sharing of his Cross, and so becomes a means of fellowship, friendship, communion with Jesus in a way that nothing else can be. It becomes a most intimate privilege and draws the one suffering right into the mystery of the Sacred Heart, which is a heart pierced by life's sorrow and life's pain.

And so the prayer ends with the triumphant note: "Blessed be your holy name." That word blessed is such a beautiful word; it expresses something very precious. We say: "That was a blessed day when I first met my friend." "I shall never cease to bless you for your goodness to me." "Bless you!" we say to someone whom we love. That is the word Bernadette used to try to express her gratitude to her Heavenly Father for his precious gift. "Blessed be your holy name."

And so, as Bernadette passed her last days on earth blessing her Heavenly Father for the cup of suffering which he gave to her, we too may be called to bear our cross in this way. If this is our situation now, or if we become ill in the future, instead of being sad or bitter because of our lot, we should try to spend the rest of our life blessing our Heavenly Father for the priceless privilege of being allowed to drink from the cup which he has given us. If we make the effort sincerely, then God will surely give us the grace to make this sacrifice.

Now, where did Bernadette learn this secret? Why was she able to offer that marvelous prayer? It was because somebody else had uttered that prayer before her.

Our Lord's agony

We can imagine that we are outside Gethsemane; the long Agony in the Garden is just over; Our Lord's enemies begin to close in upon him; they bind him and take him prisoner. St Peter draws his sword to stop the whole business because it all seemed so wrong. Why should Christ suffer and be humiliated? Why should Christ be crucified and die? Our Lord replies: "Put your sword back in its scabbard; am I not to drink the cup that the Father has given me?" (*Jn* 18:11). In the midst of the darkness of the Passion - and no greater darkness could there ever be - Our Lord looked through it all straight into Heaven and he saw in the agony of Calvary the cup which his Father was giving to his Only-Begotten Son. That which seemed so evil was in reality the Father's most precious gift to his beloved Son.

Your prayer

So if we are suffering in any way, this can become our prayer. We may well feel lonely, and our human nature will shrink from the cup. But don't forget that the perfect humanity of Jesus shrank from the dreadful ordeal he was facing till the sweat poured from him, and then there came an angel from heaven strengthening him. We may say: "Yes, but there is no angel coming to me." But if we have grasped the message of Bernadette and Lourdes, we have surely found something more wonderful than any angel. We have discovered that, despite our sufferings, we have a mother in heaven who was first our Mother of Sorrows on earth, and that she has stooped down from heaven and has taken us in her hands and supports us while her Divine Son, our Saviour, holds the cup of suffering to our lips and says: "Won't you share with me the cup that the Father has given me?" And as he says these words, Gethsemane becomes heaven, Calvary the throne of

God, and our sufferings become bearable and perhaps even for some, paradoxically, the gateway to joy.

That is what the message of Lourdes does in a way that perhaps nothing else in the world can do except Lourdes and all that Lourdes stands for. The man of the world can't understand. He shrugs dismissively and says: "Perhaps."

But our answer should be: "There is no 'perhaps' - we know." "My God, it is your will. I accept the cup that you have given me. Blessed be your holy name."

The Problem of Suffering

Am I not to drink the cup that the Father has given me?" (*Jn* 18:11)

The above text can be thought of as a sermon in its own right, and in reality it is one which anyone who is suffering must never forget, something which ought to be imprinted on their minds for ever, if their sufferings are to bear fruit.

In this text lies concealed the whole answer to the problem of suffering. It illuminates the whole problem of suffering, pain and death. What a problem it is! It lies at the root of all life's tragedy. Men and women meant for peace and joy are often overwhelmed instead with sorrow, suffering, pain, and finally death. All have to face it, for "man... breeds trouble for himself as surely as eagles fly to the height" (*Jb* 5:7). Anyone who is sick knows this only too well. Even those who are strong and have their health will almost certainly one day come to it, this problem of suffering, pain, and death. It is the problem that drives many away from God. Why should we suffer? What have we done? Can God be good if he allows this suffering? It is all such a hopeless waste; the good suffer and the wicked apparently escape.

Some people are driven to despair. Others hold on bravely, they will not give in; but they have no answer, and all is difficult and dark; they just play out time: they have no real hope. We can tell it by the way they talk. "Let the young have a good time while they can" is what they say - a pathetic philosophy. Others fling themselves more and more into pleasure because they know it is not going to last.

Almost everyone is affected by it; the sun of life goes out, the darkness overwhelms our faith, uncertainty dims our hope, and the very pain of it all quenches our love. Is there any answer? But for those who have faith, who are genuine Christians, there is a very beautiful answer. It is all in these words: "Am I not to drink the cup that the Father has given me?"

Living with God

First of all, what is the cause of all this pain? Where has it come from? Did God mean it? The answer is that pain and suffering were not part of God's original plan. God made us all to share in his life, to be one with him in a life of supernatural love, to live with him for ever with no suffering, no pain, and no death as we know death.

The Heavenly Father however, made only one condition in order that we receive this gift - and that was obedience, obedience absolute and complete. "Of the tree of the knowledge of good and evil you are not to eat" (*Gn* 2:15). This obedience was the sacrifice by which man should worship God. Our first parents disobeyed. Man fell, desiring to be independent of God, to decide for himself what is good and evil. He fell and so separated himself from the Father who loved him, and had made him because he loved him and wanted his love in return.

The result was that instead of love there arose selfishness; instead of humility, pride; instead of joy, sorrow; instead of health, sickness and death. All became chaos and confusion.

Such is the story, and indeed not merely a story but a most real and awful fact. And, all men being one, the human race being one, inseparably linked together in all its sufferings and joys, therefore the fact of this disaster makes itself felt throughout the whole race. The result of original sin is in us all. The guilt, it is true, is washed away in baptism, but its weakening effects remain. We are the victims of suffering, pain and death.

Convincing proof

Now we come to God's remedy for all this. One thing was greater than man's sin - God's love. A plan was ready. In the heart of the Holy Trinity lay an amazing answer which should be a convincing proof of God's overwhelming love for man. God the Son, the second person of the Holy Trinity, would come down and, becoming man, would take upon himself human nature and, in that human nature, would shoulder suffering, pain and death, the results of man's sin; that is to say, to lift from the shoulders of sinful humanity the burden which humanity had brought upon itself. He who was all good and had been rejected by man would do this freely for the very humanity which had rejected him. And so God came to earth.

And how did he come to earth? At the very moment of the Fall, this plan had been foreshadowed in the words: "I will make you enemies of each other: you and the woman, your offspring and her offspring. It will crush your head and you will strike its heel" (*Gn* 3:15). Our Lady was the instrument chosen by God to give us his Only-Begotten Son. At Bethlehem Mary brought forth her firstborn Son and laid him in a manger. From the very first she was drawn into the problem of pain. Her Son was to carry it on his shoulders, and she, his mother, would share it with her Son. What mother could do otherwise? From the very first there was suffering: the persecution by Herod, who sought to kill her Child; the flight into Egypt and all that that exile meant; the prophecy of Simeon: "And a sword will pierce your own soul too" (*Lk* 2:35).

But we must not linger here. We must pass on to the point where her Son, Our Blessed Lord, entered supremely into this problem of suffering, pain and death - Calvary.

Calvary, a love pact

First of all, as he approached Calvary, how did he regard it? Speaking to his disciples he said, "The Father loves me, because I lay down my life" (*Jn* 10:17). The

Father, you see, loved him because he was to die upon the Cross. On the night before he died he turned to his disciples in the Upper Room and said: "The world must be brought to know that I love the Father, and that I am doing exactly what the Father has told me. Come now, let us go" (*Jn* 14:31).

And where did he go? Straight to his Cross. Do you see the point? Calvary was a love pact between the Father and the Son. As he left the Garden of Gethsemane they closed in, led by the traitor, to seize him. Peter, impulsive Peter, drew his sword. Something must be done. This is all wrong, disaster. His master must never suffer, least of all die. Poor impetuous Peter got the whole thing completely wrong. Our Lord turned to him and said: "Put your sword back in its scabbard. Am I not to drink the cup that the Father has given me?'"(*Jn* 18:11). All the horror of Calvary - its darkness, its pain, its injustice, its cruelty, the blows, the taunts, the scourging and the wounds - so far from being something to be avoided, was the most precious gift from the Father to his Son, for thus was the world to be saved, sin to be conquered, the grave to be opened, and the way back to God secured for man.

Listen: three days later, the same voice was speaking: "I am ascending to my Father and your Father" (*Jn* 20:17). Standing by his open grave, he showed us that death was overcome; death was and is the gateway to Heaven, the key to God's heart. Those very things which are the result of man's separation from God - suffering, pain and death - are now made the very means by which man comes back to God, to everlasting life with him.

And at the foot of the Cross stands his mother. The mother of Bethlehem - now become the Mother of Sorrows - who was with her Child until the end.

Now do you see what this means for us? It means exactly the same. It means that the pain, the suffering, the death which lie before us are simply the cup which our Heavenly Father gives us.

St Paul understood

There was one person who understood this with all the vehemence of his passionate nature, and that was St Paul. He would have no half-measures. He would grasp the truth, the whole truth, about the Cross. He would make the Cross the very centre of his life. He would see to it that pain, suffering, and death, should be for him the very path to the heart of his Heavenly Father, the means to perfect union. Listen to this: "For him I have accepted the loss of everything... and I look on everything as so much rubbish if only I can have Christ... All I want is to know Christ and the power of his resurrection and to share his sufferings" (*Ph* 3:8ff).

There is the first point. It is only those who are in pain who can really understand the amazing mystery that when God himself came into the world, he chose pain and suffering. Our pain interprets his pain. Between all friends there is a link which joins them in friendship, and in our friendship with Jesus the link which joins us to our friend is our pain. As lover looks into lover's eyes and is silent and understands, so the suffering soul looking upon a suffering God needs no explanation, but is at rest.

Never again need we be lonely in our pain. Our pain can open to us a way we never realised before. It shows us that, just because of us and because of our pain, God himself chose pain, so that in it and because of it we should have him for our special friend. The very thing which seems to cut us off from the friendship of so many around us gives us another friendship for which all the friendships of the world are no recompense - the friendship of our suffering Saviour. That is the first thing.

More than friendship

But now there is something much more wonderful still, and it is this. Friendship and companionship become something more, they become union. We can not only become the special friends of Jesus through pain and suffering, but can actually become one with him so that he lives in us and we live in him.

Listen to St Paul: "I have been crucified with Christ, and I live now not with my own life but with the life of Christ who lives in me" (*Ga* 2:19). Could anything be more beautiful? With Christ we are nailed to our cross, to our suffering, to our sickness. As he hung completely dependent on his Cross, so we can be utterly dependent upon others around us, and through this very cross we become one with him, so that he lives in us, loves in us, suffers in us. We live, yet not with our own life, but with the life of Christ who lives in us. And all of this can come to us through our sufferings.

These are lessons which it is almost impossible for those who are well and strong to learn, at any rate as those who suffer can learn them. There are depths of the love of God which only pain can probe, and those depths are the special secret of the one who suffers with Christ.

A marvelous ministry

But now there is something further still. Why did Our Lord suffer? In order that he might save the souls of men. And the marvel of it all is this: that those who suffer and are sick, by offering their sufferings in union with Our Lord - with our God - by offering them in union with his Cross, can call down graces and blessings from that Cross upon other souls. We know how if one member or part of our body suffers our whole body suffers, and how if one part of our body is sick all the other parts contribute towards its healing. So in the Mystical Body of Christ, his Church, we can offer our sufferings through him who is the Head of the Body to heal the other parts or members of that Body.

See, then, what a marvelous ministry can lie before us. St Paul put it this way: "It makes me happy to suffer for you, as I am suffering now, and in my own body to do what I can to make up all that has still to be undergone by Christ for the sake of his Body, the Church" (*Col* 1:24). Could anything be more beautifully expressed? Our Lord Jesus wants our suffering for the completion of his work for souls. He stoops down to us and asks us to help him in his work of salvation.

And so, we who are sometimes tempted to think that we are no good, that we can do nothing, that we are just a bother to all our friends - we can do far more than the greatest preacher or the most learned theologian or the greatest administrator. In accepting our suffering, we are the most powerful instrument for helping the souls of others, because we are being drawn most fully into the mystery of our Saviour's Passion.

So then, for those who are ill - suffering, pain, and death, are simply the chalice which the Father is giving to every one of them, his children.

From sadness to joy

The amazing thing is that in every pilgrimage to Lourdes the greatest lessons which are learned by those who are strong and well are the lessons which are taught to them by the sick. It is the supernatural peace and patience, the supernatural joy and happiness radiating from the faces of those who are lying ill, which are often the most vivid treasure that they carry back from Lourdes. The change from sadness into joy, from discontent to peace, from weariness to radiant happiness amongst the sick is really Lourdes' greatest miracle.

God gives to each person who suffers a chalice, a chalice which may well be filled to the brim, and specially filled for each single soul with exactly the suffering which is going to perfect them and make them missionaries to those around them.

And in the centre of all this stands Our Lady on Calvary, the sword piercing her heart. It was there that Our Lord gave her to us to be our mother. Through the pangs which she suffered on Calvary she brought us forth as her children to the life of supernatural grace, she our Mother of Sorrows. And at Lourdes that same blessed mother, pierced by the sword of suffering, pain and death, leads the sick to her Son and to his Cross, to find their answer there and to hear him say: "Am I not to drink the cup that the Father has given me?" At Lourdes, Mary our mother stoops down to each one of us, her children, watching over us, loving us as we drink our cup, the cup which she drank before us at the Crucifixion of her Son.

How intimate, how intense her understanding is of all the pain of those who suffer! If her heart was pierced with a sword by the suffering of her Son, how intensely she must love all those for whom he suffered, those who - offering their sufferings in union with his, which also were her own - find in them the cup which the Father gives them.

In union with Christ

Last of all, whom did Our Lady use to draw people to Lourdes where she has showered such treasures on her children who are sick? It was Bernadette, poor and weak in health, who finally was to lie on a bed of very painful sickness, slowly dying with great suffering, while Lourdes was going from glory to glory.

When they came to Bernadette and told her the great things that were happening at the Grotto, she said "Yes, but my business is to be ill." She had no desire to return, or to receive any flattery for the wonders that were happening at Lourdes. All she desired was to drink the cup which her Heavenly Father gave her, and so penetrate to the heart of her crucified Saviour, to live a life of union with him possible only through her pain, and to die at last in the arms of her Mother of Sorrows, who all along had shown her such proofs of her love for her suffering child.

Light in the darkness

Sometimes, when people who are ill return home uncured from a pilgrimage to Lourdes they can be inclined to say: "I wish I could get the spirit of Lourdes back again. I wish I didn't have to put up with this suffering." What they ought to say, as every sick person also ought to say, are just these words: "Am I not to drink the cup that the Father has given me?" If we are able to do that we will find that our faith will revive and a supernatural hope will lift us above all our pain, or at least make it bearable. These words will be for us a light in the darkness and will give us a quiet confidence when things seem most hopeless. They will also carry us through that last great moment of death when we pass away from our weak, suffering bodies and our soul is free at last to go to Jesus and Mary.

The glory of Jesus in heaven lies in his sacred wounds, and our glory in heaven may well be that wounded body with which we have suffered so much on earth. So we should pray for the grace to be able to glory in our sufferings, and to thank God for them. We should realise that suffering is a most wonderful treasure. This is the real message of Bernadette, and Lourdes, for many people. It enables them to be glad to suffer, glad to be the child of the Mother of Sorrows, glad to be the intimate friend, a friend especially beloved, of the Man of Sorrows, Jesus Christ, perfect God and perfect Man, the world's most perfect Sufferer. "Am I not to drink the cup that the Father has given me?" Yes, Lord Jesus, may we have the grace to answer that question with an emphatic "yes".

You and your friends

If we are called to suffer then we are also meant to realise that it is through our patience and our love, our courage, happiness and joy, that we are going to show others that the suffering which has come upon us is not, as it seems to them, a thing impossible to understand which is to be stoically borne, with a hopeless resignation, but is the cup which our Father gives to us, his children, a cup filled, in reality, with blessings to the brim.

Prayer of St Bernadette

O Mary, O Mother of Sorrows!
At the foot of the Cross you received the title of our Mother. I am the child of your sorrows, the child of Calvary. O Mary, my tender Mother, behold your child at the end of her resources. Have pity on me. Obtain that I shall one day be in heaven with you.

You, who saw and felt the utter desolation of your dear Son, assist me during mine. I come to place the anguish of my heart in your heart and to draw from it strength and courage.

May I remain like you at the foot of the Cross, is such be the pleasure of your divine Son! May I begin here below, my soul united to your soul, to glorify the Lord by this perpetual homage of a perfect submission.